Threads & Friends
BOOK TEN

Rita the Right Fielder Comes Clean

by Peter J. Mulry

Copyright © 2022 Peter J. Mulry. All rights reserved. Except for brief quotations for review purposes, no part of this book may be reproduced in any form without prior written permission from the author.

Published by:
Peter J Mulry Foundation

Contact the author:
peterjmulryfoundation.org
850-221-1045

Print - ISBN: 978-1-7358638-9-4

I would like to thank several people who made this book possible - Lou Maggio, KR Lombardia, Gary Ippolito and Andy Taylor. I would also like to thank Mario Garcia, my Guardian Angel who has been with me through this endeavor. A tip of the cap to all the sponsors for their financial support.

Thanks to all who have helped me on my journey.

After a long, cold winter, Rita the Right Fielder was so glad to wake up to a warm spring morning. She couldn't wait to get outside and toss the ball around with her friends on the All-Stars team. After she got her glove, Rita grabbed a waffle from the plate her mother was just about to put on the table. "Bye, Mom!"

"Wait!" her mother said. "Aren't you supposed to study for your spelling test today?"

Rita thought studying for her spelling test sounded boring, especially when the weather was so nice. "I will when I get home."

Her mother frowned. "Okay, as long as you promise to study. You didn't do so well on the last spelling test, remember?"

Rita saw Pedro and Louie walking past her house on their way to the field. She knew her mother was right, but right now, she didn't want to study. She wanted to play baseball! "It's so warm out today and I really want to play baseball with my friends."

"Sports and friends are important, but so is your education," her mother said. "You have to keep your grades up if you want to play on the All-Stars."

Rita promised again to study and ran down the street to meet her team. The All-Stars had a great practice that day, and when Coach Threads asked if anyone wanted to stay after to practice catching, Rita was the first to volunteer. By the time she got home, she was tired and hungry. After dinner, her mother reminded her to study for her test, but when Rita tried to read the words, she ended up falling asleep.

After homeroom the next day, their teacher announced that it was time to take the spelling test. "These are all words from the book we read last week, so you should know them, especially if you've been studying. Class, get out a sheet of paper and a pencil and be ready to spell the words that I read aloud."

Everyone did as they were told. When the teacher read off the first few words, Rita wrote them down without too much trouble. The words got harder to spell as the test went on and when the teacher said, "Triumph," Rita realized she didn't know how to spell that word. It sounded like it ended in an "f", but she wasn't sure.

She squirmed in her seat. She only had a few seconds to spell the word before the teacher moved on to the next one. Rita began to panic about getting a bad grade and then not being able to play baseball. That would be the worst. What was she going to do?

She glanced over at Louie's paper, saw what he had written down, and copied the answer onto her own test. She immediately felt ashamed and mad at herself for cheating, but didn't tell the teacher about her feelings when she handed in her paper.

When Rita went to practice that afternoon, she had trouble concentrating because she was thinking about the spelling test and what she had done. She knew it was wrong, but didn't know how to make it right.

Coach Threads told the other players to practice batting so he could talk to Rita. "Is something bothering you, Rita?" he said. "You don't seem like yourself today."

Rita started to cry. "I…I…I cheated on my spelling test."

Coach Threads looked concerned. "I'm surprised you would do that. You're usually a good student."

That made Rita feel even worse. She didn't want to let her coach down. "I didn't want to study this weekend. I wanted to play baseball. And when I went to take the test, I didn't know the words. So, I looked onto Louie's paper and… and…" Rita started to cry again. "I feel terrible, Coach. I don't know what to do."

"Well, I think the answer starts with being honest. You need to tell your teacher what you did and accept whatever consequences you have."

"But, then I'll get a bad grade!" If she had too many bad grades, she wouldn't be able to play baseball. That made Rita cry even more.

"Yes, you might get a bad grade, but you will also learn a lesson about the importance of studying," Coach Threads said. "When you first learned to field balls, what happened?"

"I missed them all the time!" Rita said. "You worked with me and taught me the right way to do it, and now I can field them pretty well."

"That's because you learned from your mistakes and you did better the next time. You know what to do, Rita." Coach Threads pointed at the players who were taking turns swinging at Pedro's pitches. "Now, let's go finish practice."

Rita thought about Coach's advice while she took her turn at bat. She thought about it when she walked home, and she thought about it while she was setting the table. Coach was right. She did know what to do. "Mom, I need to tell you something," she said to her mother.

"Sure. What is it?"

"I cheated on the spelling test today." Rita sighed. "I didn't study like I promised I would and I didn't know how to spell the hard words."

Her mother looked sad. "I'm disappointed that you did that, Rita. I'm glad you told me the truth, though."

"I'm going to tell my teacher the truth, too." Rita felt better just making the decision to be honest. "If I get a bad grade, then I'm just going to have to study harder for the next spelling test. Even if the weather is good."

Her mother laughed and ruffled her hair. "Exactly."

The next day, Rita got to school early and told her teacher about what happened with the spelling test. The teacher gave Rita a zero on the test and had her serve detention that afternoon. "It's one test, Rita," the teacher said. "If you work hard, you can make up that grade, but only if you never, ever cheat again."

Rita nodded. "Lying about my test made me feel terrible. I feel much better now that I was honest."

Serving detention made Rita late for practice, but that was okay. She had done the right thing and that made her feel good about herself again. When practice was over, Rita walked up to Coach Threads. "Thank you for giving me advice yesterday."

"You're welcome. How did it turn out?"

"Exactly the way it should." Rita grinned. "I'm going to study hard next time so that I am not just a great catcher, I'm a great speller too."

Coach Threads laughed and gave Rita a hug.
"That sounds like a good idea to me.
I'm proud of you, Rita."

The smile on Rita's face got even bigger. "I'm proud of myself, too." And that, Rita realized, was the best feeling in the world.

Name:

Team:

Position:

Baseball Skills on the field:

Life Skills on the field:

Threads and his Friends is a look at "Life Skills" through Baseball shared by 10 Characters representing each baseball position on the field along with the Designated Hitter. I've always believed that most "Life Skills" are easily learned with the game of baseball.

"Life Skills" such as Responsibility, Accountability, Correct Choices, Commitment, Teamwork, Hard Work, Friendship, Confidence, Honesty, and Discipline, are all part of the tools we need to give to our youth so they can grow and prosper in the game of life. As I look at our young people today, I thought these characters might be fun for them while learning "Life Skills" and some basic fundamentals at each position.

Please have fun with it!!

I would also like to thank several people who made this book possible: Lou Maggio, KR Lombardia, Gary Ippolito and Andy Taylor. Also Mario Garcia who was my Guardian Angel in this endeavor and continues to be so. A tip of the cap to all the sponsors for their financial support.

Thanks to all who have helped me on my journey.

Peter J. Mulry

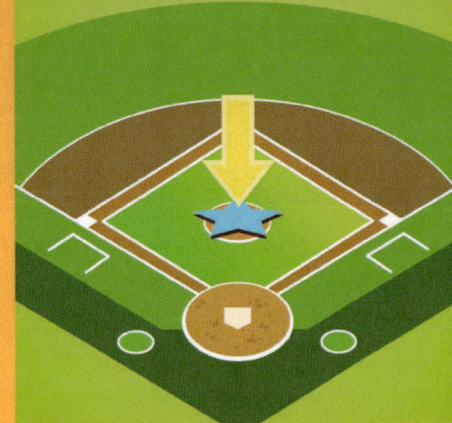

Pedro's Baseball Skills on the Field

☆ Learning how to get the right grip on a Baseball.

☆ Learning the strike zone.

☆ Learning how to get in the right position on the Pitcher's Mound.

☆ Learning wind up and proper throwing position.

☆ Learning how to pick up the Catcher's Target.

Pedro's Life Skills on the Field

Responsibility

Willingness - Pay attention to coaches.

Acceptance - Be a good teammate.

Responsive - Pay attention to all situations in a game and be alert.

Talent - Do your best and try your hardest.

Cathy
the Catcher

Cathy's Baseball Skills on the Field

☆ Learning how to put on the catcher's equipment.

☆ Learning the strike zone and where the target should go.

☆ Learning how to grip the ball.

☆ Telling teammates game situations and making her teammates aware of them.

Cathy's Life Skills on the Field

Accountability

Willingness - To learn the rules of how to play the game.

Accountability - Keeping herself and her teammates on the right track by being a leader.

Decision Making - Making the right choices.

Measurement - Knowing the rules. Knowing the count (balls, strikes, outs)

Freddie
the 1st Baseman

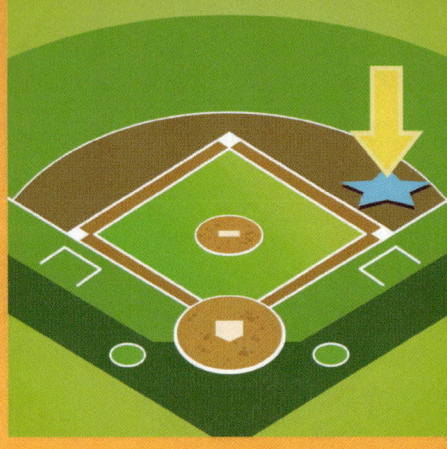

Freddie's Baseball Skills on the Field

☆ Knowing when a ground ball is hit to go to first base and put your heels on each corner of the base and be able to reach out for the ball.

☆ Learn how to use a first baseman's mitt. It will help make plays a regular glove can't—example a ball in the dirt coming from another infielder.

☆ Learning how to be the cut-off man for the balls hit to the outfield.

☆ Responsible for bunts on the right side of the field-when the situation calls for it.

Freddie's Life Skills on the Field

Correct Choices

Perception - Freddie learns by knowing what's going on every pitch during the game and what needs to be done.

Comprehension - Understand the game situation and pay attention.

Action - Taking the steps and making the choices to do what needs to be done on each play and doing it.

Manners - Know that there is a "Baseball Etiquette" when playing. "The Do's and Don'ts of the Game"

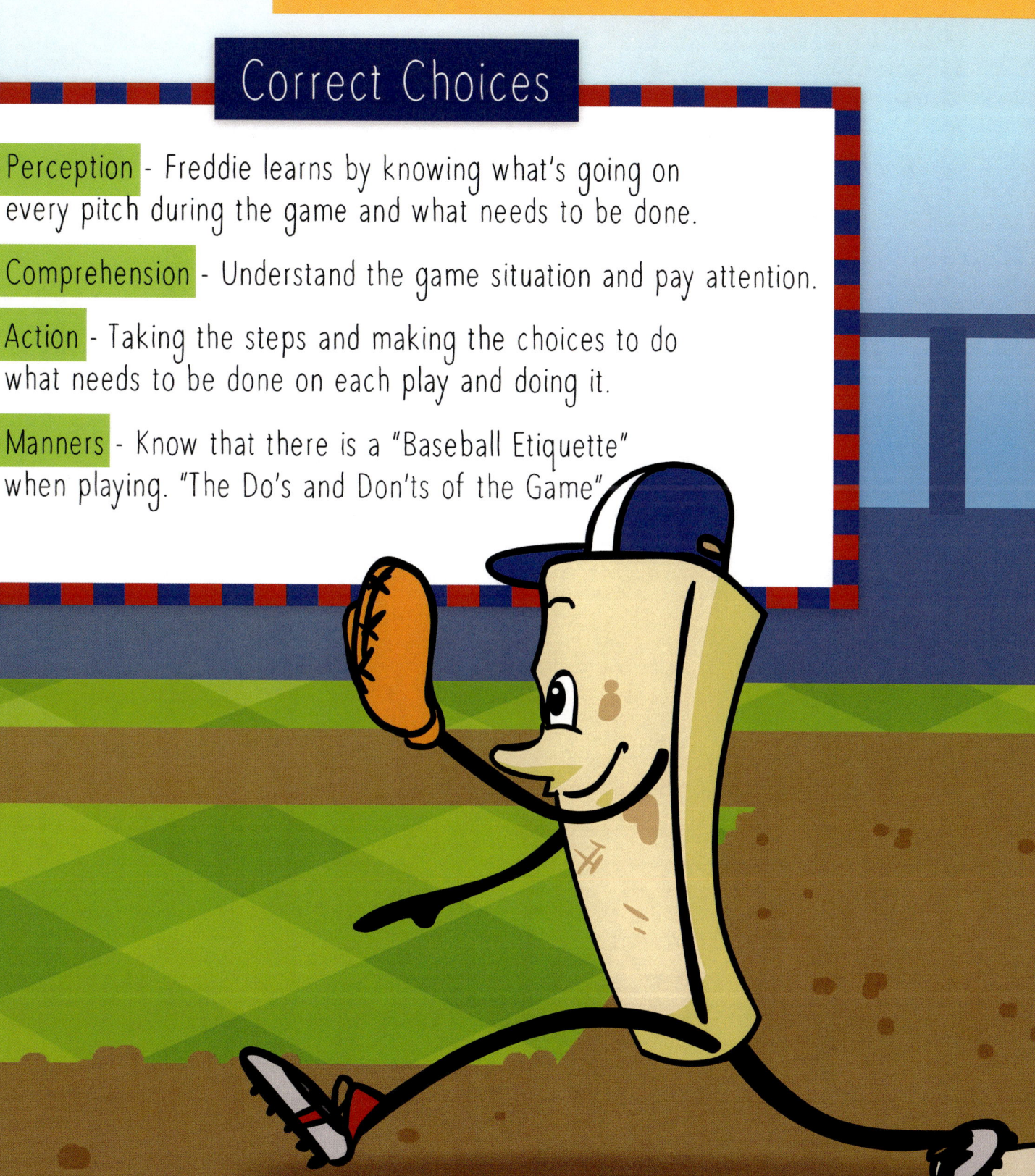

Sam
the 2nd Baseman

Sam's Baseball Skills on the Field

☆ Ground Balls hit to the 2nd baseman will go to first base.

☆ Ground balls hit to the shortstop or 3rd baseman with runners on 1st base-the 2nd baseman needs to go to second to get the throw for a force-out.

☆ In bunt plays he needs to cover first base-for the first baseman may need to field a bunt.

☆ Balls hit to the right side of the outfield—he will need to be the relay man.

Sam's Life Skills on the Field

Commitment

Conduct - Plays in a spirit of good sportsmanship.

Consistent - Belief of always giving his best on the field to himself and his team.

Sacrifice - Learning to take a little less to help one of his teammates.

Hustle - Never walk on and off the field without giving positive energy.

Samantha
the Shortstop

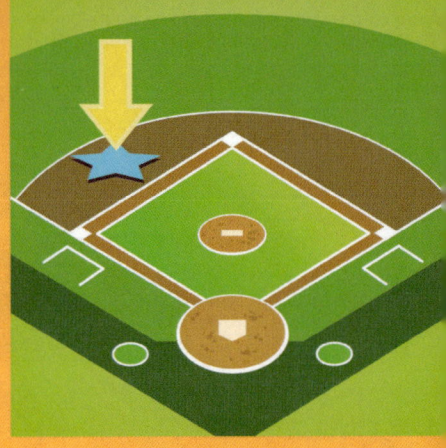

Samantha's Baseball Skills on the Field

☆ Needs the strongest throwing arm because she will make the longest throws in the infield.

☆ With a runner on first or second base and a round ball is hit to the right side she needs to cover 2nd base for a force out.

☆ In all bunt situations she needs to cover 2nd base for a possible force play.

☆ The shortstop is the relay person to the outfield from anywhere on the left side of the field.

Samantha's Life Skills on the Field

Attitude

Cooperation - She blends in with the team to get everyone to do their part. "She's a leader."

Common Goal - The common goal is to be the best we can with individuals working together to win as a team.

Respect - She knows that everyone has their own job to do and gives them encouragement to do that.

Selfless - Putting the team first-there is no "I" in team.

Gary
the 3rd Baseman

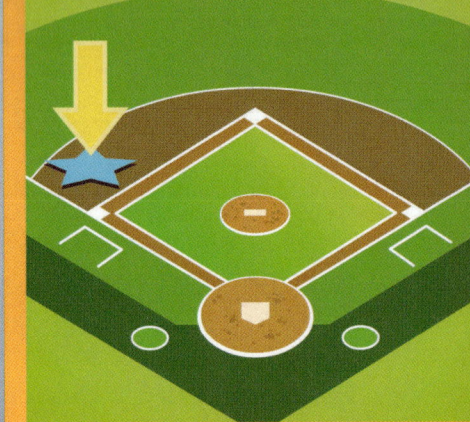

Gary's Baseball Skills on the Field

☆ The third baseman needs to have quick reactions because ground balls get to him the quickest.

☆ He needs to cover the left side on bunt plays.

☆ With a runner on first base he needs to throw to second base on ground balls for a force out.

☆ He is the relay man for balls hit into left with a runner on second base.

Gary's Life Skills on the Field

Hard Work

Discipline - Working hard every day on the field to become the best he can be. "Pay attention to the game."

Results - The end of game is determined by what you have done during the game.

Courage - Learn not to be afraid of the ball.

"Done is Never" - If you're going to be great at anything in your life you never stop working and getting better—catching ground balls every day.

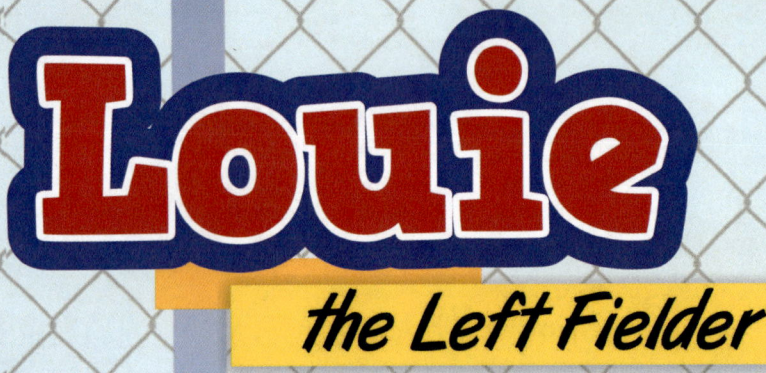

Louie
the Left Fielder

Louie's Baseball Skills on the Field

☆ Learning to catch fly balls. The best way to do this is start by using a softer ball than regular baseball.

☆ Must learn how to throw the ball a longer distance for he will make strong throws back to the infield.

☆ Needs to be taught how to long toss.

   ☆ His basic territory is from his position to the leftfield line.

   ☆ Must learn with runners on base when the ball is hit to him which base he should throw to.

Louie's Life Skills on the Field

Friendship

Trust - Trusts his coaches and teammates to do the right things and make the right decisions so his team does well.

Honesty - Being truthful to his coaches and teammates. "Louie's always honest."

Connection - Getting close to his teammates who are part of a common goal. "Lifetime contacts"

Compassion - When teammates make a mistake or a wrong play he helps them with encouraging remarks.

Chen
the Center Fielder

Chen's Baseball Skills on the Field

☆ Since he has the best view of the hitter he needs to get a good jump on the ball and be ready to back up his fellow outfielders.

☆ Runs to a spot where he feels the ball will be—"anticipate"

☆ Catches fly balls with his glove up. Good rule to learn is if ball is below the belly button the glove is down. If ball is above the belly button the glove is up.

☆ Knows every situation when runners are on base so he knows where the ball should go.

Chen's Life Skills on the Field

Confidence

Purpose - Always a reason for every play made on a baseball field.

Expecting - Chen wants every ball hit to him—he knows his position and everyone else on the field and knows what to do!

Tenacious - He lets everyone know in the outfield what the situation is before each pitch—he is the leader in the outfield.

Study - Always wanting to learn and get better.

Rita
the Right Fielder

Rita's Baseball Skills on the Field

☆ Don't be afraid to go to one knee when a ground ball is hit to you.

☆ Be ready to cover all the way to the right field line.

☆ Back up balls hit to the centerfielder and the first baseman.

☆ Always be ready with runners on base if the ball is hit to us—which base are we throwing to—the right fielder is usually the outfielder who has the best arm.

Rita's Life Skills on the Field

Honesty

Truth - Being honest with herself and the situations around her.

Integrity - Don't cheat to win.

Sincere - Being honest.

Be true to yourself in the game, if it doesn't feel right tell your coaches.

Tony
the Hitter

Tony's Baseball Skills on the Field

☆ Get in an athletic position with your body—feet spread apart knees bent where you're balanced and comfortable.

☆ Put the bat on your shoulder pick it up and put it back. These two steps will help get you started.

☆ Work with a batting tee (all ages) to practice your swing—you need to swing the bat every day.

☆ Learn how to follow the ball from the pitcher's hand as quickly as you can.

Tony's Life Skills on the Field

Discipline

Instruction - Learning to listen to coaches and instructors how to hit and get into the right hitting position.

Repetition - Learning that to be good at anything you have to do it again and again the correct way.
"Perfect practice makes perfect."

Self Control - Knowing that anything worth doing takes time and you have to have patience with yourself.
"Don't get mad."

Practice - Is the only way to get better at anything we do. However doing the right things at practice is the key.

Coach's Corner
FINANCIAL AWARENESS

Financial Goals

Spring has sprung and baseball season is back in session for the All-Star Team. Rita's mom reminded her that she needed to study for an upcoming spelling test. Instead of studying, Rita fell asleep. The next day during the test, Rita had difficulty and ended up copying the answers from a classmate.

After speaking with Coach Threads, she realized that she was in the wrong and needed to let her mom and her teacher know what she had done. Rita had to serve detention for her what she did, but both her teacher and mom were very proud of her for telling the truth.

As you learn about honesty, it's extremely important that you are honest about your financial decisions in the future. Here are some questions to think about to help guide you:

What is a bigger priority for you: saving money or investing it?

Are there special causes or organizations that you care about that you would want to donate money to?

About the Author

Pete Mulry, one of the winningest coaches in high school baseball, coached for ten years at Tampa Catholic High School, and left that job with an overall high school record of 329-39. His team won State Championships in '68, '71, '73, and '76 and a National Championship in '73. He was honored as Florida Coach of  the year in 1968, 1971, 1973 and 1976 and Nominated for National Coach of the year in 1977. Pete then moved on to the collegiate level, coaching the University of Tampa from 1978 through 1982. He also scouted for KC. Royals. He was recently honored by the *Tampa Tribune* as one of the Top 50 coaches in athletics in the Tampa Bay area. He has dedicated his life, and his foundation, the Peter J. Mulry Foundation, to teach young children life skills through sports.

Look for the next book in this fun series!

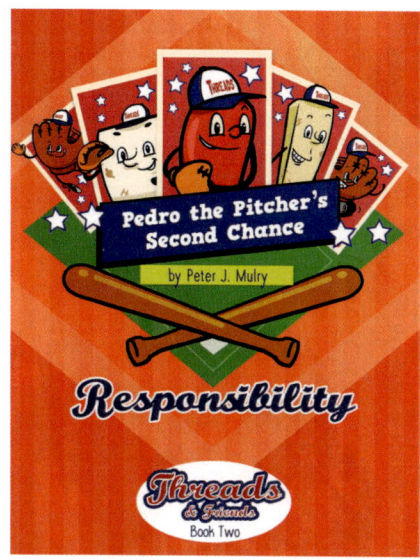

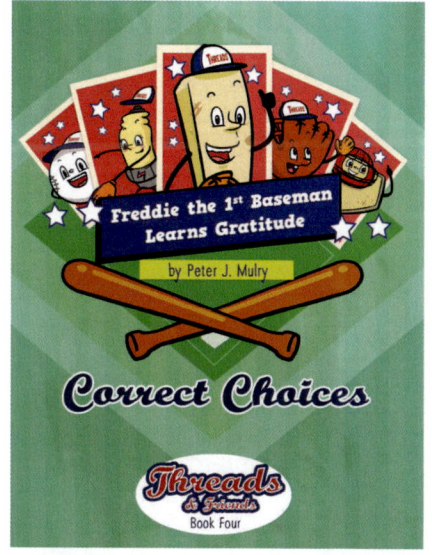

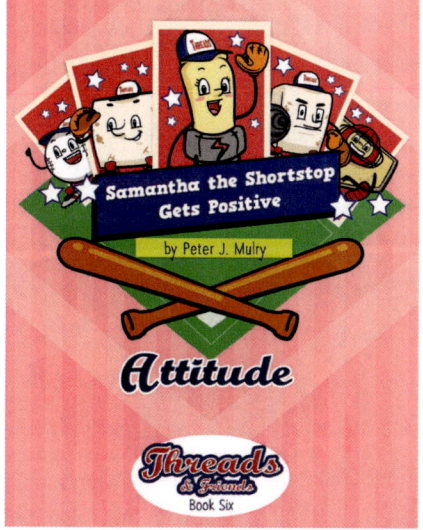

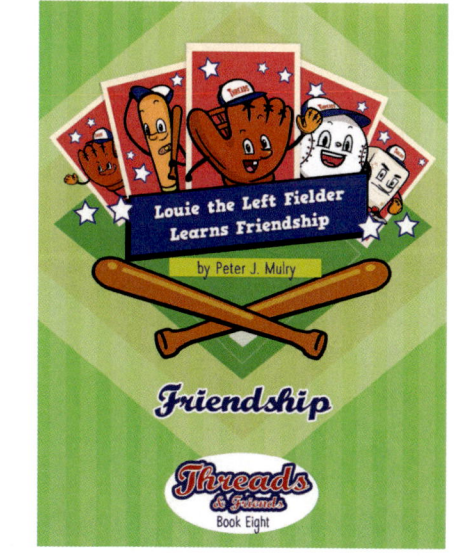

Made in the USA
Middletown, DE
10 July 2024